Vol 13

MAZE

Ages 4-6

FOR KIDS

MAZE BOOK

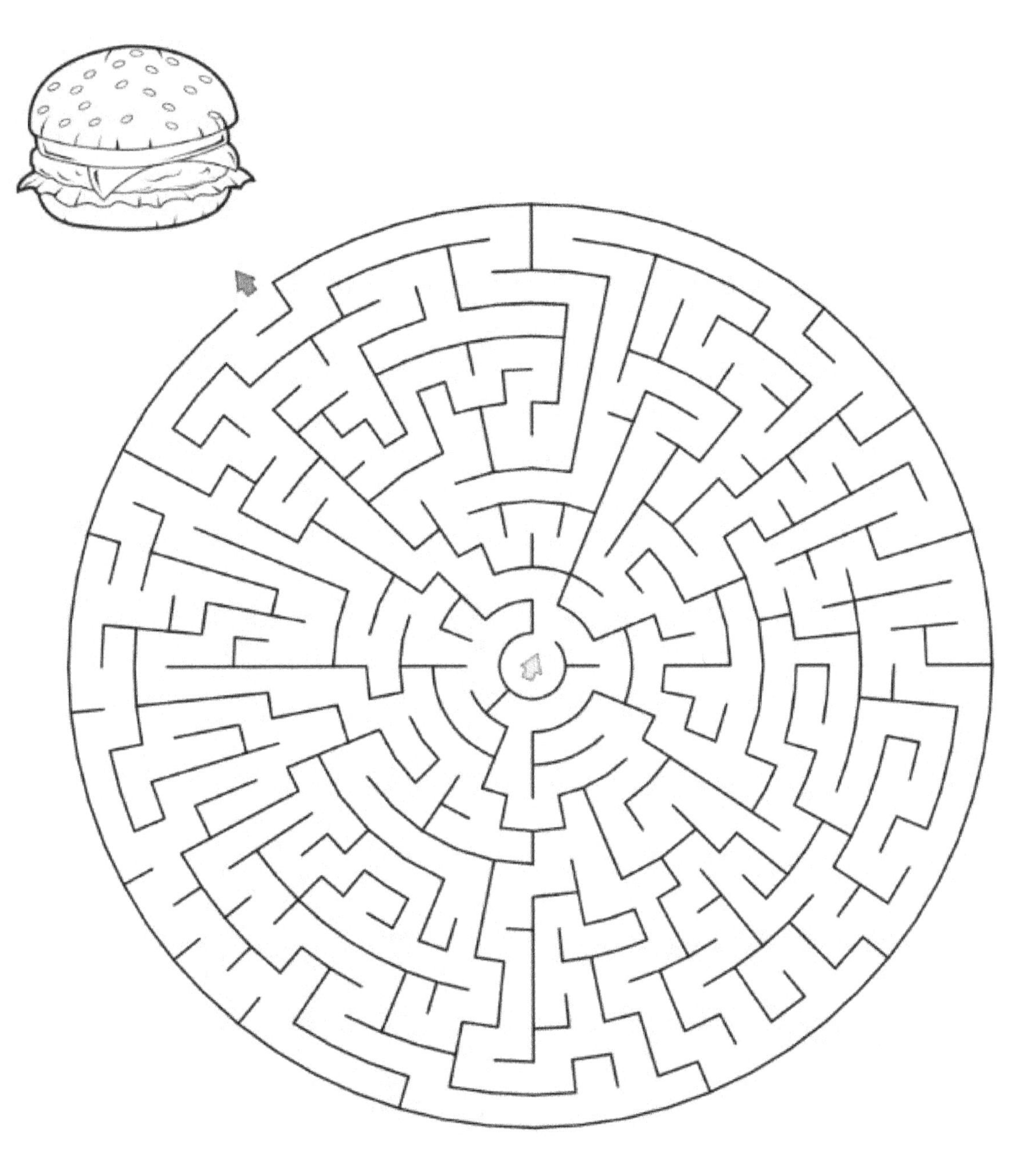

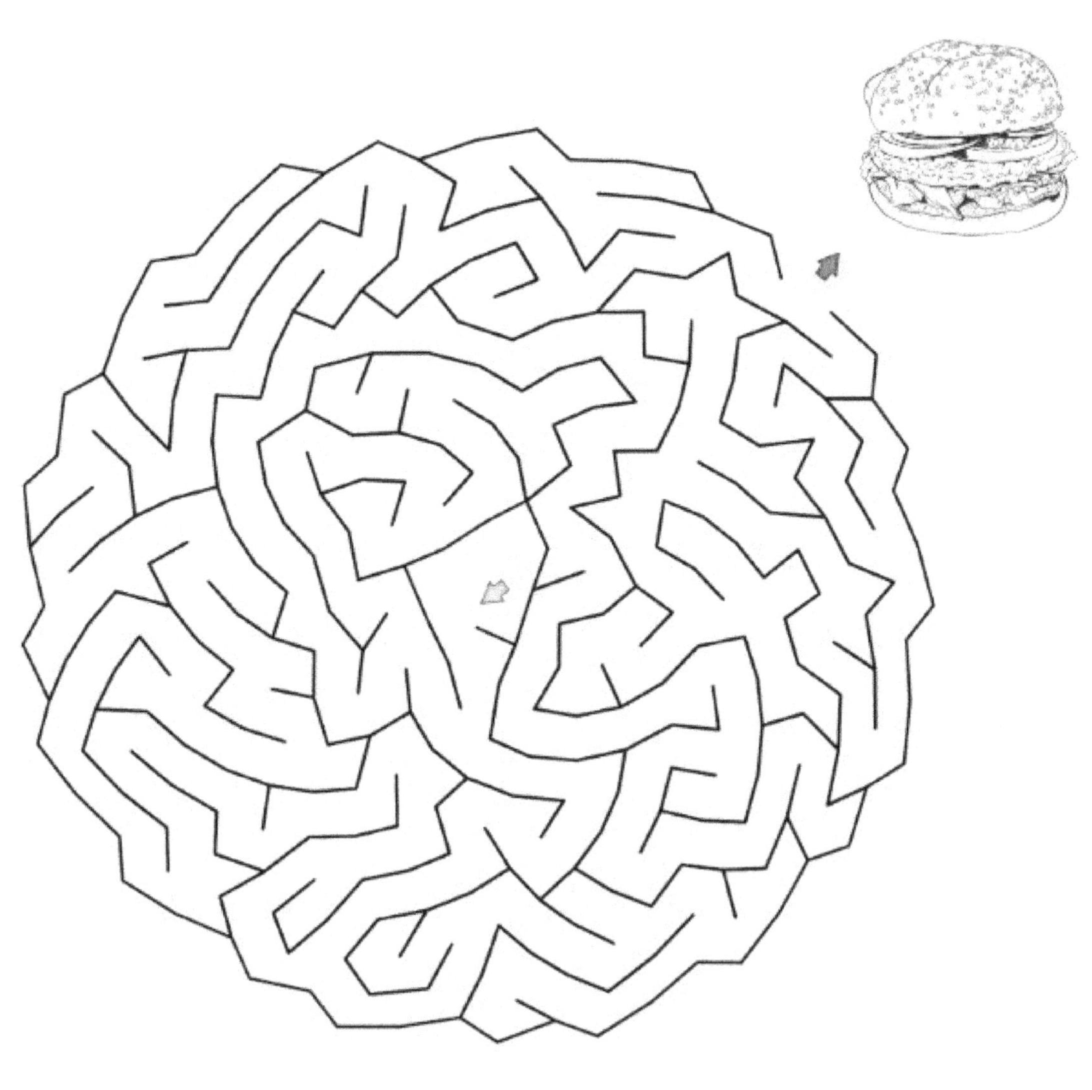

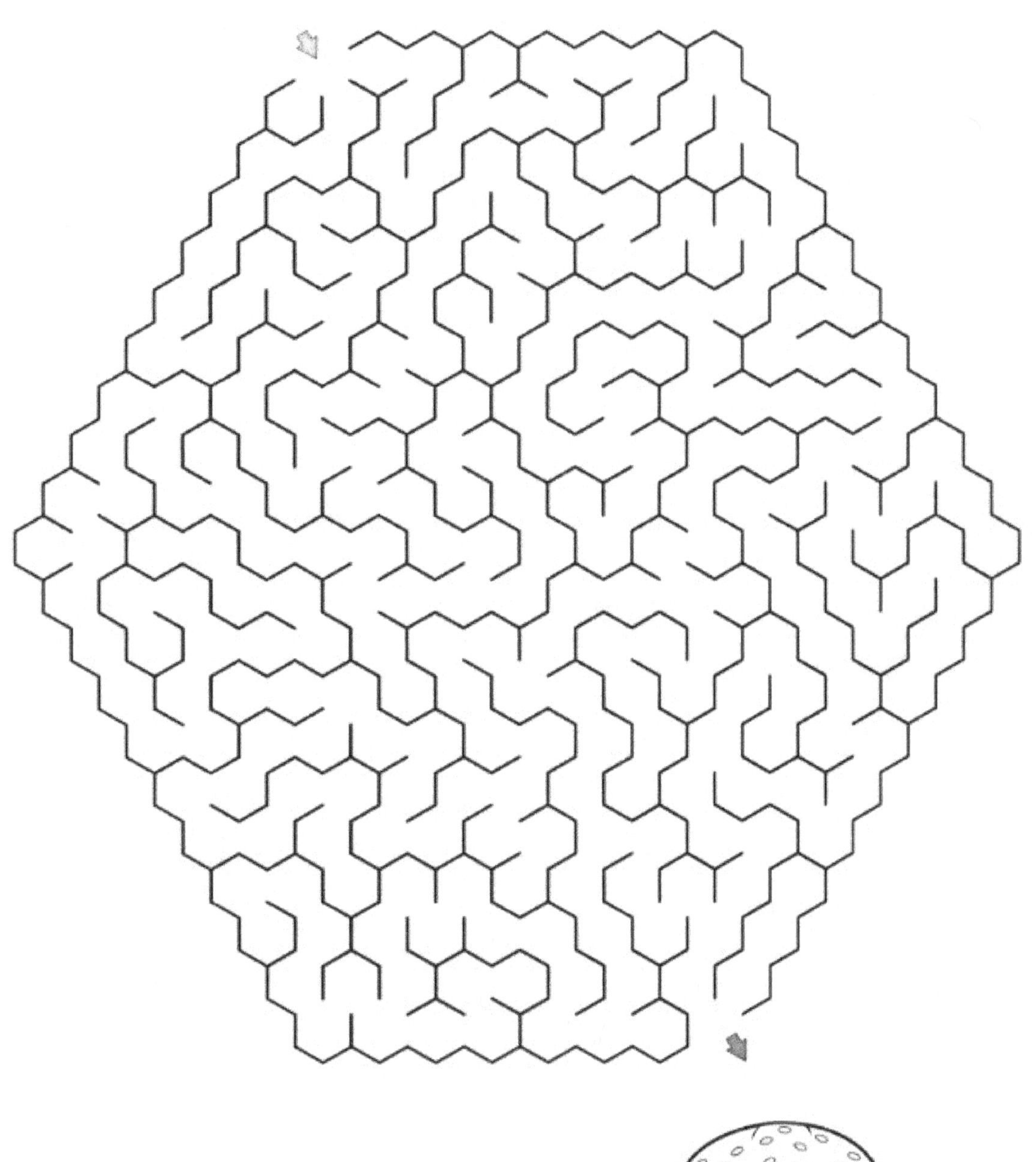

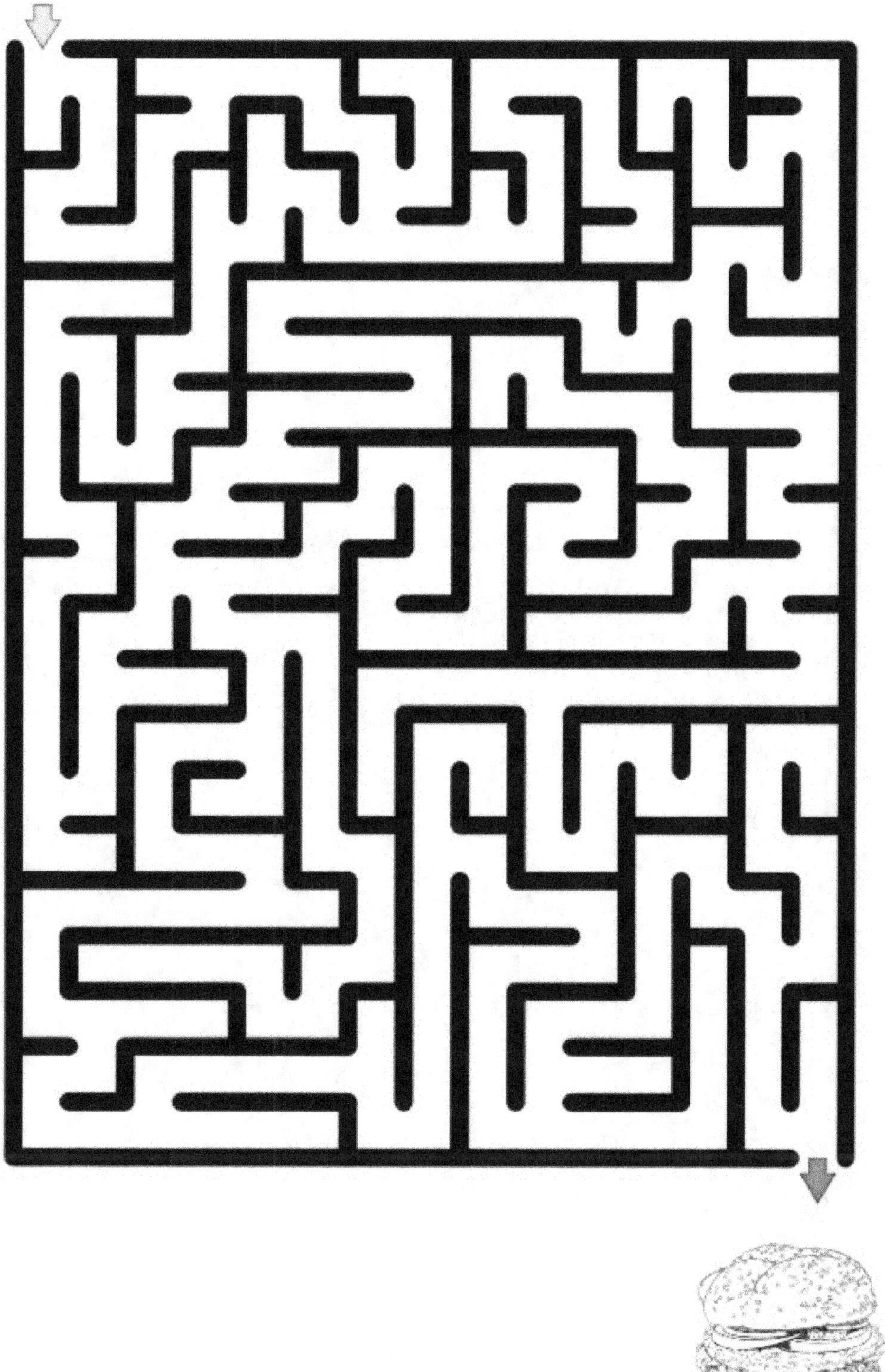

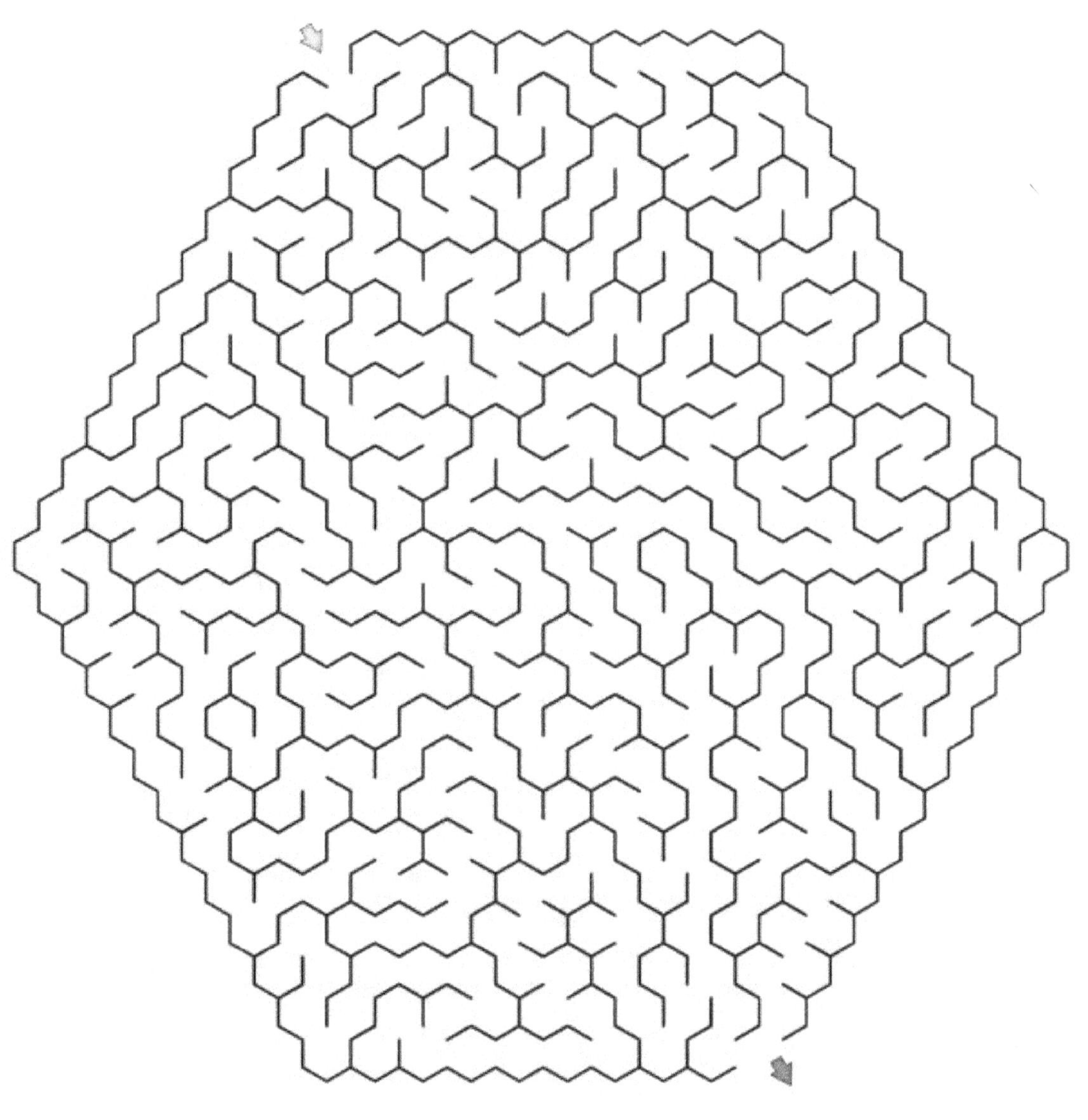

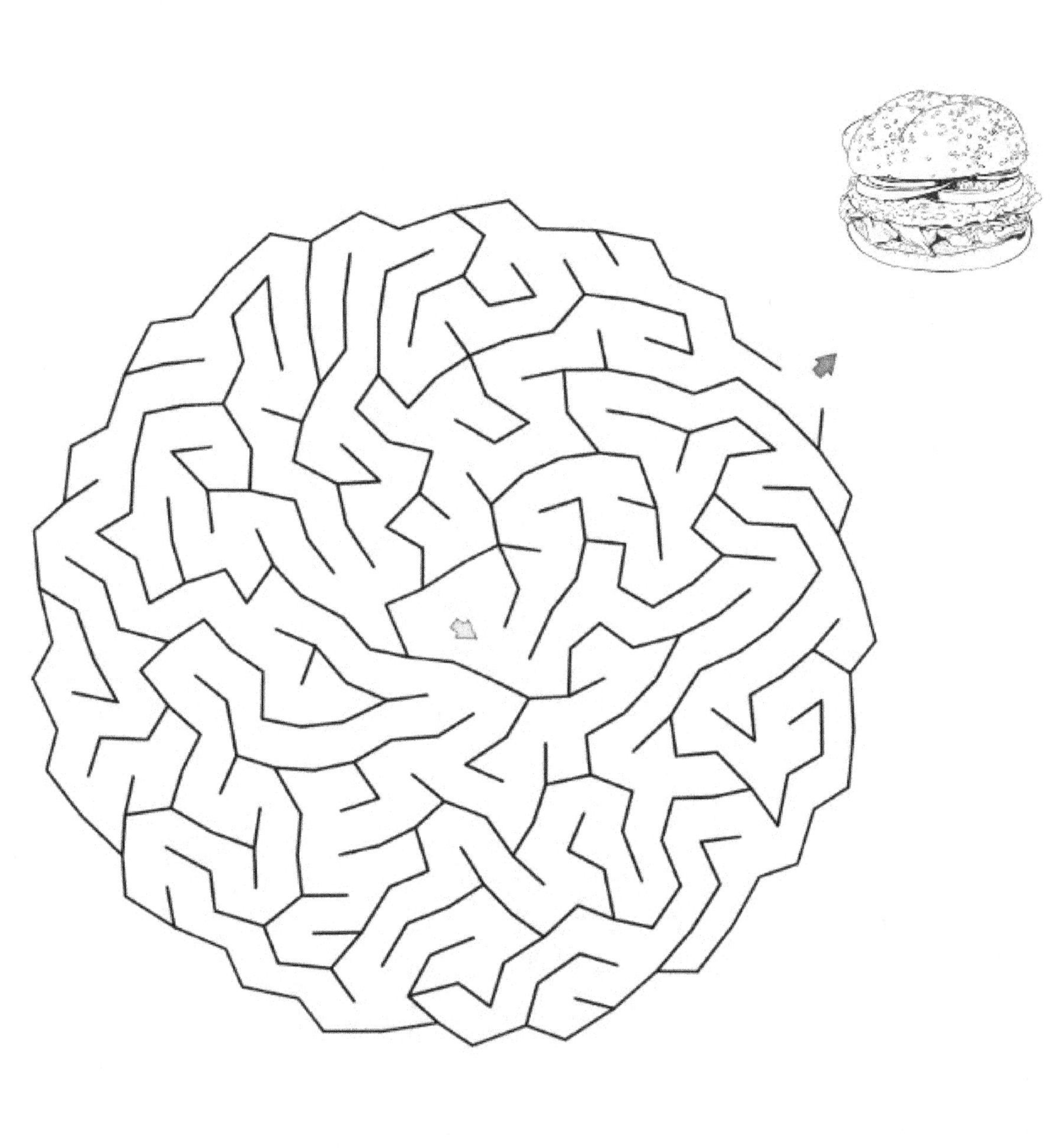

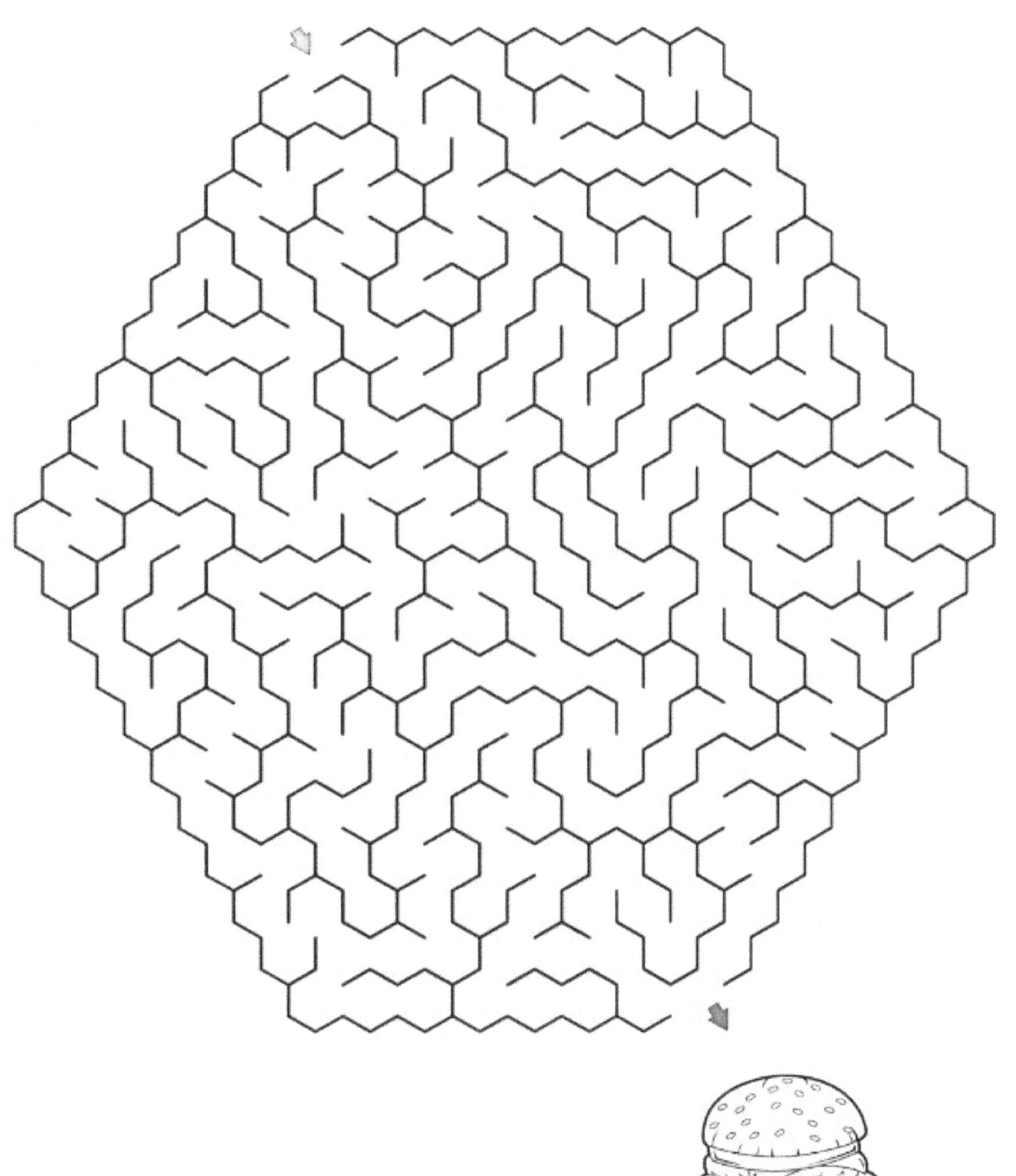

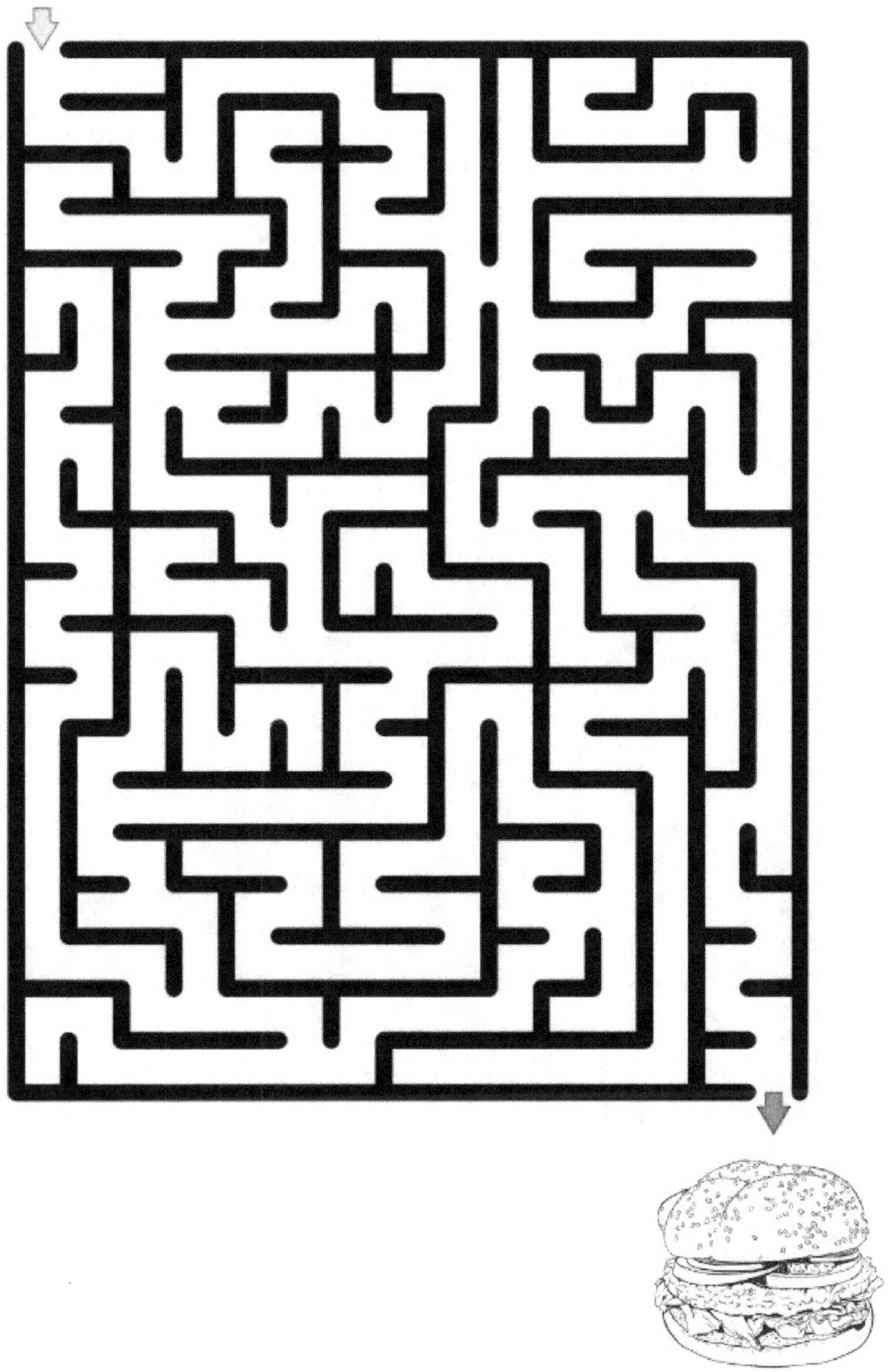

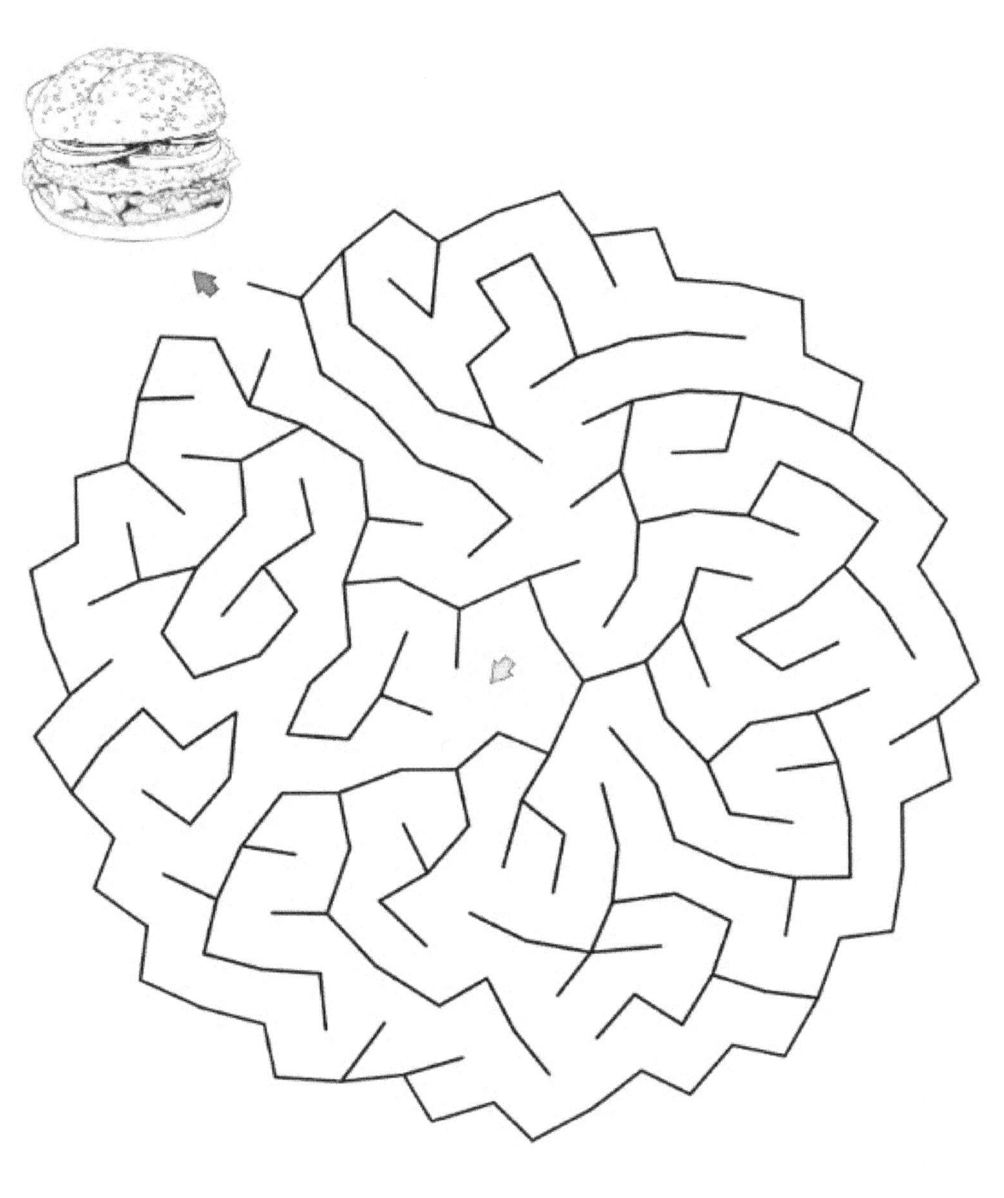

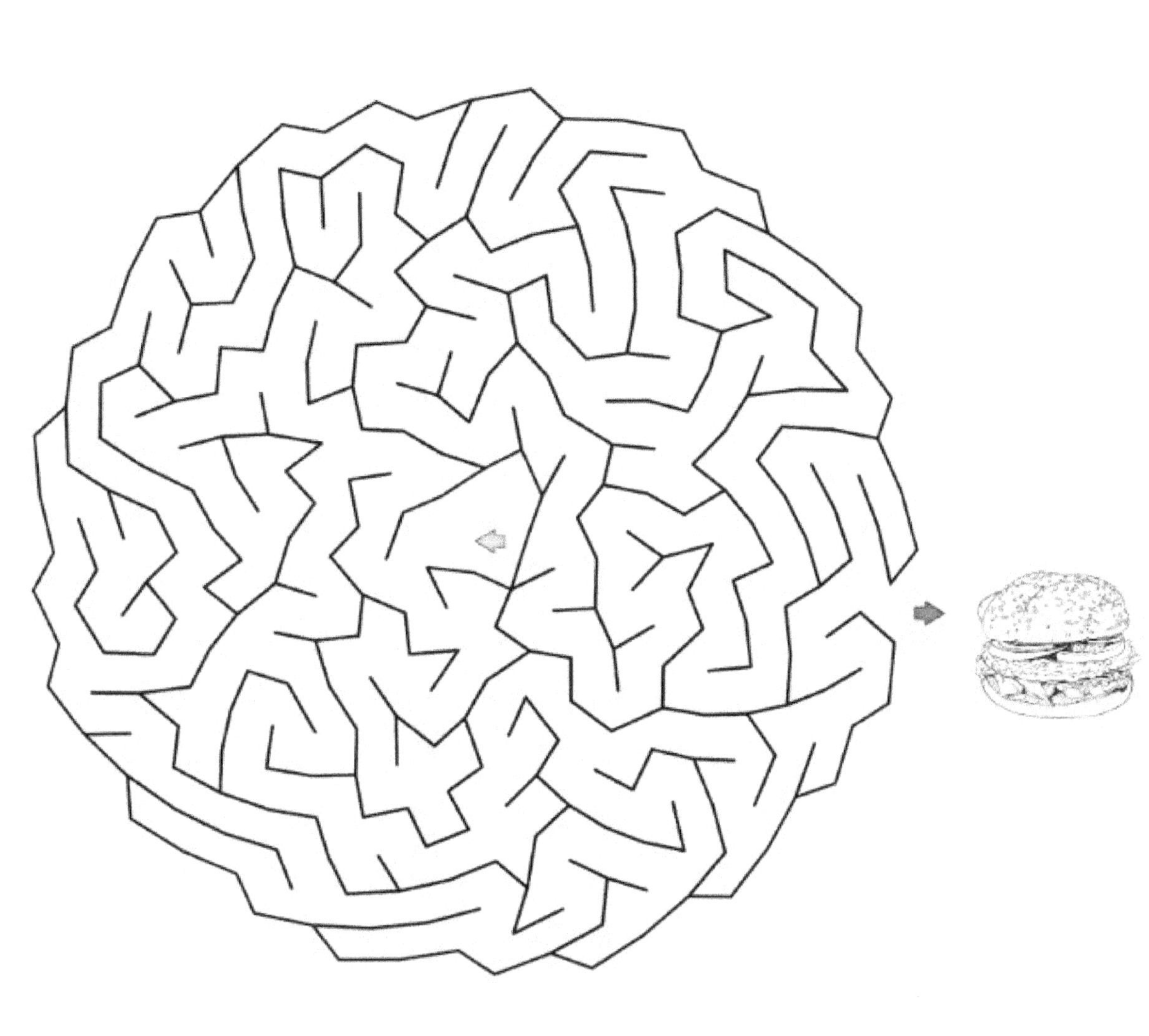

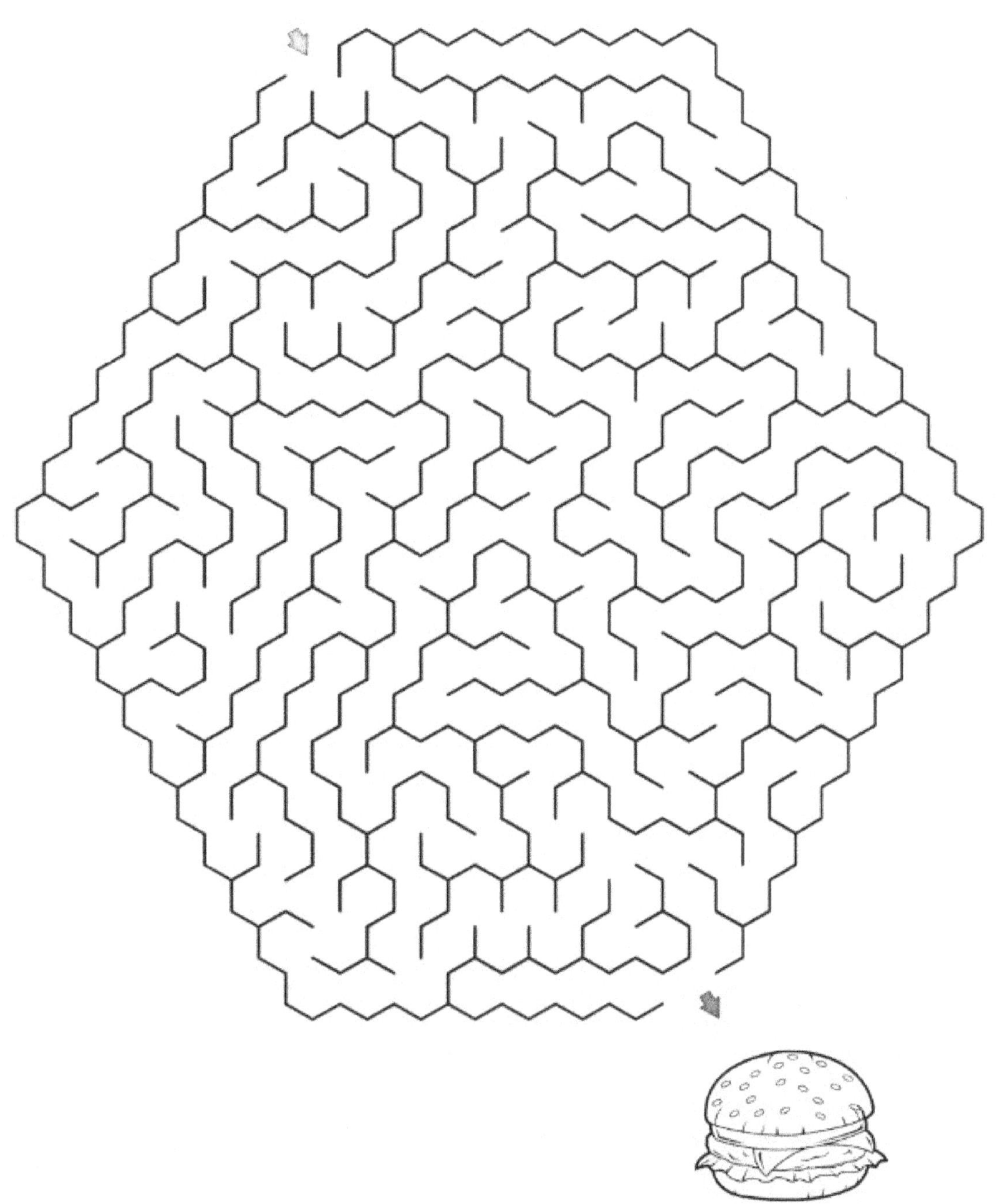

www.ingramcontent.com/pod-product-compliance
Lightning Source LLC
Chambersburg PA
CBHW081736250726
48657CB00010B/3287